Solent Yachting Scene

SOLENT YACHTING SCENE

In Bygone Years
1890-1938

DAVID COULING

STANFORD MARITIME
LONDON

Stanford Maritime Limited
Member Company of the George Philip Group
12-14 Long Acre   London WC2E 9LP

First published in Great Britain 1984
Copyright © David Couling 1984

Set in Century Textbook 10pt with Signature Black
Printed in Great Britain by
Penwell Limited
Parkwood   Callington   Cornwall

British Library Cataloguing in Publication

Couling, David
   Solent yachting scene.
   1. Sailing ships—England—Solent—
   History—Pictorial works.
   1. Title
   623.8'22'0916336   VM59

ISBN 0 540 07280 X

The photograph on the first page of this book is of
Alberta, the 160ft tender to the royal yacht *Victoria
and Albert II*. When Queen Victoria died at Osborne on
the Isle of Wight in 1901 her body was carried across
to Portsmouth in *Alberta*, accompanied by three other
royal yachts and saluted by a ten mile long line of
warships.

Foreword

The name 'Cowes' has been used for the port since the sixteenth century. Before this there was a small settlement and refuge called Shamblers, just above the floating bridge.

Some say that Cowes comes from Henry VIII's twin forts or 'cows', guarding either side of the Medina, although the place was described as 'The Cowe' in 1512 and the castles themselves were not built until 1539.

A hundred years after this, *The Ark* and *The Dove* carried the first settlers to Maryland. The port, in fact, traded extensively with the American colonies. In 1677, 4,000 hogsheads of tobacco were imported from Virginia and Customs House in East Cowes was a busy place. It was, also at a later date, the place of work of the father of Dr Arnold of Rugby; the son was born in a house in Birmingham Road, not far from the present Lallows Yard in West Cowes.

By the end of the eighteenth century, the population had risen to 2,000. The villas of retired naval men overlooked the harbour; the houses of seamen and of those who served the ships, awaiting favourable winds, in the Road. Cowes was a typical small commercial port, influenced of course by the fast growing Navy whose home was Portsmouth, not far away.

A number of Her Majesty's ships were built in Cowes. In 1780, the *Repulse*, sixty-four guns, was launched at East Cowes. She was 1,387 tons and was present at Rodney's victory at The Saints in 1782. HMS *Astrea*, thirty-two guns, captured the American forty-gun frigate *South Carolina* in the same year.

However, it was bathing, not boating, that made Cowes fashionable at the end of the eighteenth century.

Eighteen hundred and fifteen is probably the most significant date in Cowes' history. For one thing, Thomas White moved to the Medina to start a ship repairing yard which in 1857 turned into the famous Messrs John Samuel White & Co. This was probably the beginning of industrial development which was to play a growing part in the future of the town. In the same year, the Yacht Club was founded at the Thatched House Tavern in London. Meetings were held at the Medina Hotel, East Cowes during the summer, until 1825 when the Gloucester Hotel (now the Gloster) was acquired by the Club. The Hotel probably owes its name to a visit by the Duke of Gloucester and Princess Sophia in 1811. It was obviously necessary to smarten the place up a bit, for by 1816 public notice made it necessary to pass an act for 'lighting, cleansing and otherwise improving the town of West Cowes'. It also provided for a market. By gaining the patronage of the Prince Regent in 1830, the Yacht Club became the Royal Yacht Club. Three years later it changed again to the Royal Yacht Squadron, for William IV asked members to form a Naval Volunteer Force. Their larger yachts were equipped with guns. In 1857 West Cowes Castle became the headquarters. The sister fort in East Cowes was a ruin by the end of the seventeenth century.

The town developed in a peculiar way for half of it looked toward the sea and the other tried to forget all about it. The *Memorials of the Royal Yacht Squadron* record early views of this yachtsman's paradise:

> Nothing like its aspect was ever seen out of a box of Dutch toys. From the sea it looks like a heap of superior dog-kennels, which have been rolled down from the hill on which it lies and

5

brought up full on the edge of the water.

Of the social scene it was written:

> It is a no longer a small party who come down to live seafaringly, showing dresses, seeing the latest beauties and keeping clear of the hated sea.

Cowes, by this time, was the Mecca of those who preferred to be on the water rather than swimming in it. In 1851 the schooner *America* won the Round the Isle of Wight Race and started one of the world's greatest yachting epics, the America's Cup challenges.

Queen Victoria had bought Osborne a few years earlier and came to love Cowes and its surroundings. This feeling was continued by Edward VII and George V. They spent a good deal of time racing the most famous yacht of all, *Britannia*, around the Solent buoys. Prince Philip continued this with enthusiasm in *Coweslip*, *Bluebottle* and *Bloodhound*.

Recreation and leisure brought prosperity and a growing number of yacht clubs. The Island Sailing Club was formed in 1889. The Royal London founded in 1838, moved to Cowes in 1854. The Royal Corinthian took over the house that had belonged to the redoubtable Rosa Lewis of the famous Connaught Hotel. Finally, the Cowes Corinthian was established in 1952.

Earlier, this change in the pattern of life had brought John Nash, the architect, who built East Cowes Castle. About the same time, in 1799, Lord Henry Seymour commissioned Wyatt to design Norris Castle, a little east of the entrance of the Medina. Overlooking Cowes on the site of an earlier house, not surprisingly known as Belle View, is Northwood House, built in 1837 and now the home of the Cowes District Council, in the early twentieth century it housed a community of Benedictine nuns for a short time.

Cowes has always been a place full of characters. Mr Joseph Weld challenged Lord Anglesey to a race. Lord Anglesey accepted, saying that if he was beaten he would burn his yacht *Pearl* when he returned to harbour. At about the same period, one blackball excluded a prospective member from the Squadron. An applicant, the owner of a large black schooner armed with twelve guns, on learning his fate anchored on the Royal Yacht Squadron line and despatched a boat to the Castle with the message that if the man whom he had supposed to have been responsible did not come out and apologise to him on his own quarter-deck, he would open fire. At first the alleged blackballer refused, but finally sent an apologetic note after being reminded of the inconvenience of a bombardment during dinner.

The town would not be the place it is today if it weren't for Uffa Fox, who started building his dinghies up the Medina on a pensioned-off chain ferry. An islander first and foremost, he used to refer to England during the war as 'our gallant ally'.

Cowes is full of history and full of memories, whether recorded or merely retold in the marina. The best way back is through photographs and the waters of Cowes must be among the most photographed and photogenic in the world. Cowes can claim to be the birthplace of yachting photography and of the new creativity that brought this to a fine art form, in great part through the famous firm of William Kirk & Son. There is no need to emphasise this fact, for the pages that follow do more than convince: they bring back the history, the life and the magnetic attraction of the yachtsman's Mecca.

Maldwin Drummond
Chairman of the Maritime Trust

Introduction

'We are Much Pleased'

In 1980 I was fortunate enough to have my book *Steam Yachts* published, the bulk of the illustrations coming from the Kirk collection of glass plates which I was asked to restore in 1976. The collection of plates fell into two groups, steam yachts and sail, and after the publication of the first book I determined to see the second part of the Kirk collection on sail published. Happily this has now been achieved, and it gives an opportunity for those who are interested in the history of yachting to view the undoubted excellence of this maritime photographer's craft. However, it is also a sad time for me as my work on the collection has now come to an end. It has been a period which I have much enjoyed, with the restoring and printing of the plates and searching out the necessary dates concerned with individual yachts. The collection must have been a magnificent one when in its original state. I handled some thousand plates, but apart from this number I understand that there were a further three sections. One is at Cowes, Isle of Wight, another section was apparently sold, while there is talk of a last quarter stored somewhere on the Island. Imagine, if you would, if the collection were to be in its entirety what a wealth of beautiful photographs it would surely contain, in addition to the importance historically. Sadly this is not to be, but this sorry state of affairs only leads me to believe that there should be a National Museum devoted to the art of the maritime photographer. Perhaps before collections such as Kirk's are distributed to the four winds this may one day be possible, thereby saving work of historical importance for the nation to enjoy.

In the golden age of yachting there were many aspiring amateur photographers who took to the sea in order to capture the magnificent vessels which slipped in and out of port during the height of the season. Along the South Coast giants of the art emerged to delight both yacht owners and the public alike with their craftsmanship: Debenham, G. West & Son, Beken, and W.U. Kirk & Sons were the early pioneers. William Kirk came to the Isle of Wight in 1879, buying the premises at 67 High Street, Cowes where he sold general fancy goods and photographic views. By 1888 he had moved the business with his family to Bath Road, Cowes where he established himself as a leading maritime photographer. Sometime after the First World War William Kirk, now in failing health, handed over the business to his son Edgar though no doubt he kept a keen eye on it until he died in January 1928. The firm, still known as W.U. Kirk & Son, carried on under Edgar's direction until the outbreak of the Second World War when it finally came to an end.

It is almost impossible to imagine the difficulties encountered when photographers of this period went afloat in order to shoot vessels either at their moorings or underway. Plate cameras taking 10 by 8 inch glass plates were used and once they were loaded in the back of the camera one was in effect working blind, as the image of the subject could not be seen while taking the exposure. While Kirk left no record as to how he exposed his glass plates, it is reasonable to assume that his procedure would have been the following. On finding a suitable vessel to photograph he would have set up his plate camera on a sturdy tripod. With the aid of a large black cloth over the back of the camera and his head to cut out the sunlight, he would view the subject through a ground-glass screen on the back of the camera and by moving the bellows attached to the lens it could be brought into focus. The ground-glass screen was attached to the camera by means of a frame and hinges and this could be swung open in order to place a loaded dark slide into the back, the next step after focussing. From this point on Kirk would have been working blind, having no view of his subject through the lens. Setting the lens to the correct aperture and the shutter to the right speed, he would withdraw the dark slide sheath covering the plate and look at his subject to see if it had moved: if not, then he would trip the shutter and take the exposure.

With moving subjects the procedure was almost the same except that one would have to focus on a point which the vessel would pass. When all had been made ready, he would wait until she was at that point and then make the exposure. In time to come, viewing lenses were attached to plate cameras which allowed the photographer to see his subject all the time, making work a good deal easier.

One can only applaud the magnificence of detail and accuracy of his work. Today taking photographs is a relatively simple matter, with the introduction of film as opposed to glass plates and with small cameras. But there is little doubt in my mind that the quality of the old marine photographs far outshines much work done today.

Photographers now talk of fast films, emulsion speeds and shutter speeds in excess of a thousandth of a second, but Kirk and his contemporaries had none of this; even so he was the first maritime photographer to produce a print of a yacht in motion, taken in 1881. Later he was successful in capturing the Royal Yacht *Alberta* steaming into Cowes at ten knots with Queen Victoria on board. The picture appears on the first page of this book. It was shown to Her Majesty, who said 'We are much pleased with it'. We too should be 'much pleased' with William and Edgar Kirk's work for it gives us a unique glimpse of a bygone era when the very best of maritime craftsmanship sailed in the Solent waters.

David Couling

Acknowledgements

I am most grateful to the following for their help and kindness in providing me with information and photographs to include in this book.

Mr Kirk of Cyprus

Mr L.J. Mitchell BA, FLA, Director of Cultural Services, Newport, Isle of Wight

Mr John White

Mrs Harrison and the staff of the Cowes Maritime Museum

Mr Roy Brinton of the County Records Office, Isle of Wight

Mr Christopher Nicholson

Mr Bernard Cox

Mr Ian Dear

Mrs J Couling

My gratitude is particularly due to Maldwin Drummond JP, DL, Chairman of the Maritime Trust, for his generous help and encouragement while working on this book.

Author's Note

While I have endeavoured to give a brief account of the various craft illustrated in this book, the main purpose of this volume is simply to enjoy the art of the marine photographer.

I would hope that in years to come it may be possible to establish a permanent display of marine photographers' work, so that all may have the chance to study and enjoy their pictures. In order to build up a comprehensive collection I would be grateful to hear from anyone who has old photographic equipment of the period covered in this book and also glass plates, films or photographs. Such information may be sent to David Couling, c/o The Editor, Stanford Maritime Ltd, 12-14 Long Acre, London WC2E 9LP, England.

Lady Hermione

A Class One boat well heeled over and possibly shipping water into her cockpit. The photograph, taken in 1897, gives a fine impression of the little 18-footer cutting through the water.

Ghosting In

Sailing into Cowes after a day's racing. The 22ft 9in yawl was built at Forrest & Son, Wivenhoe in 1889 for F.G. Sheffield.

Circus Girl

One of the Redwing class in 1898. Redwings are still raced today, although they are now Bermudan rigged. The class was started in 1896, and the rules allow any rig of 200 sq ft total area on the one-design hulls.

The End of a Season

A group of racers display their prize flags at Cowes in 1898.

Downwind Start

Two-Raters start on the run during a race in
the early 1900s. In the background a Second
Class cruiser lies at anchor, as Guardship,
and to the right of the photograph is the
training ship HMS *Northampton*.

Moonbeam

Moonbeam, seen passing the Royal Yacht
Squadron, was designed and built by
William Fife at Fairlie in Scotland in 1858.
She was 49ft 9in long, 25 tons TM and was
owned by Charles P. Johnson.

Kothko

The little yawl *Kothko* setting her spinnaker on a sailing afternoon out from Cowes. A small cruising boat, she boasts a furling jib which was well advanced for the turn of the century. Today such sails have come back into fashion.

Britannia

The black-hulled cutter *Britannia* was designed by G.L. Watson & Co of Glasgow and built there at D. & W. Henderson's yard in 1892-3. This picture of her was probably taken around 1899. She became recognised as having a classic and wholesome hull form, which retains its attractiveness and influence today. Her dimensions were 121ft overall length, 87ft on the waterline, 24ft beam and 15ft draft. The Prince of Wales (later King Edward VII) and then George V took a serious interest in the sport and she was raced hard, becoming one of the most successful racing yachts ever. Her last season was in 1935.

Fan-Tan

Unfortunately, little is known about this 'Chinese lugger'. However, she must have caused quite a stir with her combination of conventional headsail and 'junk' rig. *Fan-Tan* was built in Poole, Dorset in 1889 by J. Allan to a design by L. Mackenzie. Her owners were a Mr Ashton and a Mr Kilner. She was 45ft 1in long, 9ft 5in beam, drew 9ft 5in and was 17 tons TM.

Primrose

A striking pose for a small yawl. She is carrying two clinker-built boats one of which seems to be rather too large for her. The four rows of reef points are also rather rare. *Primrose*'s skipper stands by the tiller while her hand stands forward of the mainsail.

Upwind Start

The start of a one-design race in May 1901.

Asthore

This auxiliary schooner was designed and built by Wm. Fife & Sons at Fairlie in 1901.

She was 85ft overall, 18ft 2in beam, 11ft draft and 118 tons TM. Her first owner was Sir Walter Rosan, Bart. Over her long career she changed owners many times and also had several names, including *Adele, Sunshine, Roseneath, Maria Stella* and *Sunshine.* She ceased to appear in *Lloyds Register of Yachts* after 1946.

From the mainmast forward, the hull and lower part of the sails is in sharp focus, but she is sailing fast and towards her stern and farther aloft her motion has blurred the image slightly.

Valdora

Taken on August 3, 1903 in her first season after delivery from her builders, Wm. Fife. She was owned by the well known yachtsman Sir William Portal. This famous yawl, later to become a ketch, won the King's Cup in 1922 and again in 1924. She was 79ft 9in overall but raced on handicap with the giants of her era, including *Creole*, *Namara*, *Maid Marian*, *Cicely*, *Brynhild*, *Wendur*, *Cariad* and *Britannia*. Sir William, a director of the South Western Railway Company,

became a keen racing man and would say of the Royal Yacht Squadron at Cowes that it was like being at home.

Namara

The 102 ton auxiliary yawl *Namara* on a lumpy day in August 1903. She was composite built with a paraffin motor and constructed by D. & W. Henderson of Glasgow in 1894 to a design by G.L. Watson. She raced in the German Emperor's Cup Race from Dover to Heligoland in 1903, though she was one of the small yachts. It was something of a gathering of giants, the entry ranging from the schooner *Cicely*, 263 tons to the much smaller cutter *Fiona*, 80 tons. *Namara* at 81ft 3in overall length lay in the smaller half of the fleet of ten yachts, racing together on handicap.

Cariad

Built for the Fourth Earl of Dunraven in 1903. During her remarkable career she won the King's Cup in 1905, 1910, 1912 and 1921. During 1929 and 1930 while under the ownership of the Rt. Hon. John Gretton, CBE she again took this prize. The ketch was 94ft 7in overall, 153 tons TM, and of composite (wood and metal) construction by Summers & Payne of Southampton.

Another view of the Earl of Dunraven's *Cariad*, passing a Royal Navy Guardship during Cowes Week in the early 1900s.

Thelma

Three fine studies of the birth of the 20-Rater *Thelma*. In the first photograph her composite construction is clearly visible: metal frames, floors and reinforcement in way of the mast step and keel, with wood elsewhere. The cutter was designed by Wm. Fife Jun. and launched from C. Hansen & Sons' yard at West Cowes on May 24, 1894. Note the delightful custom of festooning the bows with flowers before launching.

Bow-Wow

A 1-Rater ready for racing in 1895.

Hester

The new 60-Rater gaff cutter on a calm day in May 1895. It is a little unusual to see ratlines up the shrouds. Her anchor is convenient for dropping if she has to kedge in the light airs, but if the breeze got up it would be restowed so that the chain would not damage her topsides. *Hester* was designed by Wm. Fife Jun. and built in Cowes by C. Hanson & Sons.

Forty-Raters

A perfect photograph on a perfect day as three 40-Rater cutters race in the Solent on June 15, 1895. They are *Caress* (70ft 5in), *Carina* (69ft 5in) and *Isolde* (71ft 5in), which is also seen racing with *Corsair* in a 1926 photograph in this book.

Mehallah

Of the many photographs I have had the
pleasure of viewing and researching for this
book, this one of the 1-Rater *Mehallah* sums
up the sheer joy of sailing. It was taken in
June 1895.

Nimble

The little Customs launch *Nimble* coming in after making her rounds, in June 1906. Many motor launches of this type were built on the Island by J. Samuel White & Sons.

Corsair and Isolde

A fine photograph of the two 40-Raters just after starting a race in June 1896. *Corsair*, 60 tons, was at one time owned by Rear-Admiral the Hon. Victor Montague, who owned two other famous 40-Raters during his lifetime, *Vendetta* and *Carina*. With *Corsair* he won the Queen's Cup and was the first English yacht to race and win at Kiel in Germany.

Isolde also appears with *Carina* in an earlier picture in this collection. She was owned by Peter Donaldson and should not be confused with the German 20-Rater *Isolde* owned by Baron Zedwitz.

On the Mooring

Kirk's firm made and sold a number of post-cards in Cowes Week and during the rest of the year. This one shows King Edward VII on board his yacht *Britannia* at Cowes around 1906. During her 43 year career, she took part in 635 races of which she won 231.

Meteor II

This fine cutter was built for the German Emperor, Kaiser Wilhelm II, and came out in 1896. Like *Britannia*, she was designed by Watson and built at Henderson's yard; she shows a similar pleasing form and proportions though she was slightly larger and could carry a greater sail area. She raced at Cowes as well as in German regattas; manned by a British crew, she won every race she entered in German waters.

Spanish Royal Yacht

King Alphonso XIII of Spain on board his steam yacht *Giralda*, circa 1909. She had been built by the Fairfield Shipbuilding & Engineering Co of Glasgow. The Spanish government bought her in 1898 from her original American owner, Col. MacCarmont. The steel twin-screw yacht was a three-masted schooner of 1,664 tons, 289ft long and 35ft beam: an impressive sight during Cowes Week. The King was a keen yachtsman and also owned the 10 Metre *Tenina*.

Alphonso XIII had succeeded in 1902 and was constitutional monarch in a period of great tension and change in Spain and her colonies. He went into exile in 1931, and was the last king until his grandson Juan Carlos was named by General Franco to be heir to the throne and chief of state.

Below Decks

The smoking room of the 71ft auxiliary schooner *Cambria*. On the left can be seen the chart locker with a chart on top, and there is a telltale compass in the deckhead so that those below could see at a glance what course was being steered. At this time she was fitted with gas lighting, though later on electric lighting was installed. She was built in 1904 by Phillips & Son of Dartmouth.

Owner and Guests

Lunch on board *Cambria*, with the owner Mr
Cobb and his guests. Entertaining on board
the big sailing yachts was lavish, even at
sea.

Hauled Out

One of the Saunders yard buildings on the
Isle of Wight, circa 1911. A launch rests on
her cradle, ready to slide back into the
water.

White Heather II

The illustration is reproduced from one of the many postcards of famous yachts which Kirk made for sale to the general public. *White Heather* was built at Fairlie by Wm. Fife & Sons in 1907 and was owned by Lord Waring. She was one of the famous 'big class' racers, being 95ft 6in long and 179 tons TM. When all sails were set she carried around 8,000 sq ft of canvas. Her spinnaker is pulling her along in this view.

Thomas Lipton

A portrait taken while Lipton was on board his motor yacht *Erin*, in 1901. He was to build five challengers for the America's Cup, each named *Shamrock*, in the period 1899-1930, but all were beaten by the American Cup defenders. However, his efforts made him one of the most widely-known men in Britain.

Shamrock II Dismasted

On May 22, 1901 Shamrock II lost her metal
mast, which crashed down while King
Edward VII was on board as a guest of
Thomas Lipton. Here the crew examine the
wreckage while she is towed back to the yard.

Meteor IV

Although the Kaiser's earlier *Meteors* had been built in Britain or the USA and were sailed by English captains and mainly English crews, *Meteor IV* achieved his long-term plan to develop truly German crews and yachts into top-class competitors. She was built in 1909 in steel by Krupp at Kiel to a design by Max Oerst, and was quite successful racing in England and Germany though often beaten by *Westward*. She was sold in 1913 and her successor *Meteor V* only raced for a short time in 1914 before the outbreak of war. (ca 1910-13.)

Alcedo

Interiors of the steam yacht built as *Veglia* in 1895 for Baron Nicholas de Rothschild. The photographs were taken during a refit by Camper & Nicholson sometime between 1906 and 1917; she was then owned by G.W.C. Drexel and renamed *Alcedo.* In the First World War she was taken over by the U.S. Navy and with other large yachts did convoy work in the English Channel and Biscay. In November 1917 she was sunk by a German torpedo.

The 960 ton *Veglia* was 275ft long overall, 238ft on the waterline and had a beam of 31ft. Her large size allowed the accommodation to be arranged in large spaces, and the style of furnishing makes no concessions to being for a seagoing vessel.

ABOVE: Saloon, looking into dining saloon.
UPPER RIGHT: Library.
LOWER RIGHT: Dining saloon.

45

ABOVE: Smoking room.

UPPER RIGHT: Stateroom.

LOWER RIGHT: Doctor's cabin, lower down
in the hull.

Downwind Start

The start of a West Solent Class race, in enough wind for mainsails to be reefed. These pretty little yachts were mainly owned by members of the Royal Lymington Yacht Club. The date is unknown but it is thought that the picture was taken around 1920.

Thermopylae

A yacht owned by the celebrated sailmaker W. Ratsey, who enjoyed many successes in her. Built to the International 6 Metre Rule, *Thermopylae* was constructed by Anker & Jensen in 1921 and had a sail area of 483 sq ft. The photograph was taken on July 28, 1926.

Creole, ex **Vira**

This beautiful 167ft schooner was designed and built by Camper & Nicholson at Gosport for the tremendously wealthy American Alexander Cochran, whose earlier *Westward* is shown elsewhere in this collection. On viewing her for the first time, shortly before her completion in 1927, Cochran was so intimidated by the size and power of the rig, and then a very sick man, that he had all three masts lopped by fifteen feet, necessitating unstepping them and altering all the rigging and sails. On a second visit he asked for a further fifteen feet to be taken off, thus ruining her appearance. Cochran died shortly afterwards and *Vira* was sold, to begin a varied career typical of many large schooners. She was bought by Major E.W. Pope who renamed her *Creole* and sailed so regularly between the Royal Yacht Squadron at Cowes and Southampton that she acquired the nickname 'Pope's ferry'. At some date after this picture was taken Sir Connor Guthrie, her next owner, had her remasted and rerigged

to the original design. As *Magic Circle* she did mine depolarising work during the Second World War and afterwards was sold to a German shipping company. Again *Creole*, she was owned for years by Stavros Niarchos, the Greek shipowner, who again restored her rig after her gear had been destroyed in a bombing raid on Gosport. She is now run as a sail training ship in Denmark, and her three tall masts of identical height make her instantly recognisable.

Lulworth and Britannia

Two famous big class yachts racing through the Solent. *Lulworth* (left) was designed and built by White Brothers of Southampton; she was a typical 23 Metre of her day and 95ft long, 21ft 8in beam, 13ft 9in draft and 186 tons TM. Her sails were made by Ratsey's at Gosport. Today she no longer sails for she has become a houseboat on the Hamble River.

Lulworth and Shamrock

Two mighty yachts of an era now sadly passed, crossing the Solent. *Lulworth* (2) was built in 1920 for R.H. Lee and was originally *Terpsichore*. Her name was changed to *Lulworth* when she was bought by Herbert Weld in 1924. The two yachts were similar in length at 95ft 5in and 96ft 6in respectively, but *Lulworth* drew 13ft 9in against *Shamrock*'s 11ft 2in.

Shamrock was constructed in 1908 also as a 23 Metre, for the famous yachting enthusiast Sir Thomas Lipton. He owned six *Shamrocks* in all; *I* to *V* were built expressly to challenge for the America's Cup between 1899 and 1930 but sadly all were to fail. The 23 Metre *Shamrock* was used extensively for racing in home waters. Of the big class yachts she proved a very successful craft, winning a high proportion of her races.

La Cigale, ex Sea Foam

Although this 12 x 10 glass plate was badly damaged by damp, it still retains much of its original quality. The yacht was originally *Sea Foam*, built by Camper & Nicholson and 122ft long with a displacement of 295 tons. She was a topsail schooner with auxiliary power and designed for extended cruising. At sea, her crew would have been larger than the group of twenty shown here.

Narcissus

In 1905 *Narcissus* was built for E. Miller Mundy by the Fairfield Ship & Engineering Co of Glasgow. She was one of the many large steam yachts of the period which were fitted out with all the various rooms, furnishings and comfort of a large house.

However in both wars *Narcissus* changed from a luxury yacht into a fighting vessel. In the First World War she was renamed HMS *Narcissus II* and armed with two twelve-pounders. She fired on and claimed a hit on UB49; at the time the Royal Navy disallowed the hit but it is known that the German U-boat had to put into Cadiz for repairs before returning to service.

In 1928-9 she underwent a major refit at Camper & Nicholson's during which her turbines and boilers were removed and replaced with Sulzer diesel engines. These pictures were taken for the yard during that time, and show part of her accommodation.

The Second War again saw her in the Navy, this time as HMS *Gieve*. In 1940 she took part in the rescue of British troops from Dunkirk, bringing home some two thousand men on her first trip across to the beaches. On returning to Dunkirk she hit a mine and was lost with many of her crew.

Deck saloon.

Two views of the study. Beyond the open
door the edge of the balustrade at the top of
the companionway is just visible.

Companionway.

Dining saloon, which was on a lower deck.

UPPER LEFT: The owner's wife's writing cabin.

LOWER LEFT: Looking from the writing cabin towards the boudoir.

BELOW: On deck, looking forward.

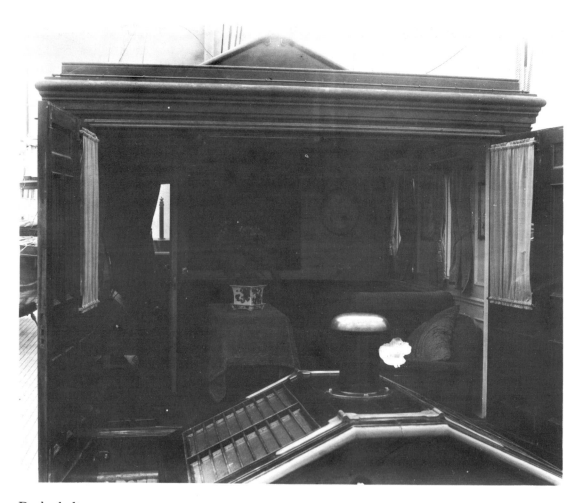

Deck shelter.

Sagitta and Aile

Camper & Nicholson built this 8 Metre Class sloop to the design of C.E. Nicholson in 1929. She was owned by the Nicholson family and gave them many happy hours of racing. In his book *Great Years in Yachting*, C.E. Nicholson said of this class, 'Here was a fine fleet of delightful yachts with an unusually pronounced sense of friendship among owners and skippers.' Her close competitor in this 1931 picture is the French yacht *Aile*.

Oonah

One of the popular West Solent Class, which had evolved from the demand by numerous yachtsmen who required an excellent sea boat with accommodation, unlike the 6 Metre yachts which though larger did not have any. The photograph was taken on July 9, 1929 when *Oonah* was owned by Major W.T. Towers-Clark, MC. The 28ft 6in cutter was built by the Berthon Boat Co in Lymington.

Paula IV

I feel sure that both Kirk and *Paula IV*'s owner Kenneth Preston would have been very happy with this shot of her at speed. She was a 6 Metre (ex *Echo*) and built by the Bute Slip Dock Co in 1924.

Braemar II

The 91ft *Braemar II* was launched in 1929 at J. Samuel White's yard at East Cowes for George Paxton. She was built in galvanized steel, displaced 122 tons and was considered a good design in her time. The second picture shows her after being fitted out. Interestingly, she is still in commission today.

Grey Fox

In 1929 when the picture was taken *Grey Fox* was owned by the Rev G.F. Eyre. She is an interesting craft in that she was a converted RNLI Lifeboat, No. 515. G.L. Watson designed her and she was built at the Thames Iron Works, London in 1902. Lifeboats were great favourites for conversion to yachts, and it is good to see No. 515 given a new lease of life. A sturdy craft, she was 35ft long, 9ft 1in beam, 4ft 4in draft and powered by two two-cylinder petrol engines.

Rhona and Iris

The 12 Metre yachts *Rhona* K7and *Iris* K6, taken in the Solent on August 5, 1929. *Rhona* was owned by the Earl of Essex and built by Wm. Fife & Son in 1927. *Iris* was built in 1926 at Port Bannatyne by the Bute Slip Dock Co, and was owned by Benjamin S. Guinness.

LEFT: Another view of the 12 Metre *Iris*, taken two days later.

Harmony

Harmony was built on the Isle of Wight in 1925 by Woodnutt & Co and designed by A. Westmacott. The V on her sail is the insignia of the Solent Sunbeam Class, still raced today. The little 21ft 5in sloop (ex *Whiskey*) was owned by Mrs Hugh Collins and Lt Col G.H. Hodgkinson. The photograph was taken on August 8, 1929.

Moonbeam, Mariquita and The Lady Anne

Three giants battling it out off Cowes in August 1929. From left, they are *Moonbeam* (8), *Mariquita* (20) and *The Lady Anne* (10). At the end of the First World War many thought the day of big-yacht racing was drawing to a close, but with King George V bringing out his *Britannia* again it acquired a new impetus and survived until 1937.

Moonbeam

The gaff cutter *Moonbeam*, designed and built at Wm. Fife & Sons' yard for Charles Johnson, was launched in 1920. Many had thought that after the First World War the racing of larger yachts would decline, due to their high costs of building and maintenance. However, in *Moonbeam*'s handicap class of above 70 tons this 79ft 5in cutter was only of average size in comparison with other yachts.

The Lady Anne

An excellent photograph of *The Lady Anne* cutting through the water, taken on August 8, 1929. She was in the 15 Metre Class and though relatively small (64ft long), in her day she raced on handicap with much bigger yachts.

Cariad

This pilot cutter, then owned by Cmdr H.F. Nash, took part in the 1929 Fastnet Race but retired before rounding the Rock. That year *Jolie Brise* won in a time of 18 days, 18 hours. An unusual aspect of *Cariad* was her squaresail, which she carried at the start of the race when there was very little wind around. She was built in 1905 in Cardiff by R. Hambly.

Westward

Known as the Herreshoff flyer, the schooner *Westward* was designed by N.G. Herreshoff and built in steel for Alexander S. Cochran of New York by the Herreshoff Manufacturing Co, to be launched in March 1910. After that year she never returned to American waters, and came to rank with *Britannia* in popularity with the general public; she was one of the best known of the Big Class yachts to race around our shores, and a great rival of the King's yacht. Her racing career lasted from 1910 to 1935 though she had to race on handicap against much newer yachts, and she was laid up in 1938.

Britannia's end came in 1936 when she was scuttled off the Isle of Wight after King George V's death, and *Westward* was to have the same fate. With the death of her last owner T.B. Davis in 1942, *Westward* was left to his family. As she was not going to be raced again the family offered her to several training institutions with the proviso that she be properly maintained. In the postwar period there were no offers to take the schooner over, and thus a clause in Davis's will came into effect that required her to be scuttled. On July 15, 1947 *Westward* was towed out to the Hurd Deep off the Casquets and scuttled by an explosive charge. At the time there was consternation over this act, but surely it was far better for her to die that way than to rot away on some lonely mud berth.

Britannia

FOLLOWING PAGE
Without question, *Britannia* was the most successful big racing cutter ever built. King George proved to be as much in love with her as his father had been, and in 1930-1 in order to keep the yacht competitive in the Big Class he had her gaff rig replaced with a Bermudan mainsail, seen here. It was set on a 175ft hollow spruce spar, and the photo shows some of the complex arrangement of shrouds and stays used to support it, rigging which led to their being called 'Marconi' masts when they first appeared.

Stella Maris II

On a more modest scale, the little 31 ft *Stella Maris* seems a fine craft to potter around the creeks and harbours of the South Coast of England. She was really a motor-sailer, built in 1920 by Lander's of St Ives and powered by a petrol-paraffin engine. The photograph was taken in June 1930 when she was owned by J. Pazolt. It is interesting to see that even though she is small *Stella Maris* had a paid hand, who can be seen by the mast.

Kathleen

A fine picture of this 65-footer, taken as she cruises in the Solent in June 1930. *Kathleen* was then owned by Herbert E. West, and had been built by Camper & Nicholson in 1925.

Arlette

The very pretty *Arlette* out for a day's sailing on July 23, 1932. A local vessel, she was designed and built by Camper & Nicholson at Gosport in 1930. The 48ft 9in yacht was owned by Martine de Selincourt.

Xarifa

Mr M. Singer of New York had several yachts built with the name *Xarifa*, though they were never distinguished by number. The three-masted auxiliary schooner shown here was built in 1927 by White's, and in 1930 they launched a steam yacht for the same owner. She was to serve in the Second World War as a naval vessel under the name *Black Bear*.

White Owl

A fine lee-side study of the yawl *White Owl* taken on September 1, 1930. She was then owned by Lt Col A.F. Watt, DSO, and had been built by Gann & Palmer of Teignmouth in 1912. As an auxiliary, this 56-footer had a four-cylinder paraffin engine.

Peter Nell

The twin-engined 60ft *Peter Nell*, from Thornycroft's yard, built in 1924.

Dorina and Moonbeam

Dorina (left) and *Moonbeam* racing in Stanswood Bay off the Isle of Wight on June 31, 1931. One is almost reminded of the song 'Stately as Two Galleons' as these two beautiful gaff cutters cross the Bay. *Dorina* was built by Wm. Fife in 1909 to the International 15 Metre Rules and in 1931 she was owned by J.S. Highfield of Southampton. Her length was 63ft and she had a Thames Measurement of 50 tons. The larger *Moonbeam* (79ft 5in) was also a Fife boat and raced in the handicap class for yachts above 70 tons.

Wander Bird

This heavily built cruising schooner is seen coming into Cowes in August 1931.

Brise-Vent

The French entry at the start of the 1931 Fastnet Race. She was built at Boulogne in 1928 for George Fortin by Lefeure's and designed by T. Bertrand. *Brise-Vent* came ninth in the race, taking 16 days, 21 hours.

Eve

The steel launch *Eve* was built in 1874 by Thornycrofts at Chiswick. Her long and very narrow lines were for speed; she was 44ft x 9in x 6ft 2in x 2ft 7in.

Mistress

The American yacht *Mistress* before the start of the 1931 Fastnet Race. She was joined by two other schooners from the U.S.A., *Amberjack II* and *Water Gypsy*. Although *Mistress* was owned by George E. Roosevelt, she was then skippered by the well known amateur Sherman Hoyt. The famous *Dorade* won the race in 15 days, 17 hours, 17 minutes with *Mistress* in third place and only 24 minutes, 7 seconds slower.

Patience

The Nicholson designed cutter *Patience*, another competitor in the 1931 Fastnet Race. The day was very hot and after the starting gun it took seventy minutes for the last boat to clear the starting line. The race was closely fought with *Patience* coming in sixth.

Highland Light

One of two American cutters taking part in the 1931 Fastnet Race. *Highland Light* took fourth place.

Maitenes II and Ilex

Although the 1931 Fastnet Race started in a calm, it was marked by very bad weather with winds reaching Force 10. On board *Maitenes II* tragedy struck the joint owners, Lt W.B. Luard and Col Hudson, when the latter was lost overboard. Luard later reported, 'We threw a lifebuoy as soon as possible and swung her off in the hope that the sea anchor warp would ride towards him, that possibly he might be forced into the drogue itself, and that somehow we might be able to haul him in. He succeeded in grasping the warp but it was torn from his hands and, encumbered by seaboots and oilskins, he sank at once.'

Naula

The handsome auxiliary *Naula* was built by J. Fay & Co at Southampton in 1903, originally as a yawl; she was converted to ketch rig in 1923 and given a petrol engine in 1927. The photographs were taken in 1931.

Dorade

The crew of *Dorade* at the start of the 1931
Fastnet, which they won. Olin Stephens is
at the left: this yacht's success gave a great
boost to his reputation as a designer.

Unity

The 8 Metre *Unity* came from the famous
Scottish yard of Wm. Fife & Sons in 1928.
Jointly owned by B.W. and F.R.W. Preston,
she is seen here proudly displaying her end
of season prize flags on September 23, 1931.

Gladys and Gone Away

The little X class one-design craft were raced by the Royal Motor Yacht Club, Poole Yacht Club, Lymington Yacht Club and Parkstone Yacht Club. *Gladys* was typical of her type, 17ft 8in x 6ft x 3ft 1in; she was built by Woodnutt & Co in 1913 and designed by A. Westmacott. The photograph, (LEFT) taken in 1932, shows her owner Stanley Steel at the tiller.

Gone Away (RIGHT) was also taken in the summer of 1932. Xs are still raced today.

Marigold

The cutter *Marigold* was launched in 1892 from the Camper & Nicholson yard at Gosport. At the time of the photograph, 1932, she was owned by Sir Noel T. Kershaw, KCB and had a four-cylinder Parsons engine; very probably the rig shown is not her original one.

Fay

The Solent Sunbeam *Fay*, built in 1927 in the Woodnutt & Co yard. She was owned by Mrs G.M. Reynolds and the photograph was taken on June 9, 1932.

Manou

Manou ex *Araok* was built in wood at Paimpol in 1912 and has the lines of a sturdy working boat. She was 93ft 8in x 24ft 6in x 10ft 2in draft and 223 tons TM. Her owner was Georges Boureois when this photograph was taken in June 1932.

Harkaway

This West Solent one-design was owned by J.J. Morgan in 1930 when the photograph was taken. She is still sailed today.

Lucie

The American 6 Metre *Lucie* (ex *Akaba*) in 1932, her successful year when she and three other American Sixes defeated the British in home waters during the bi-annual races, in which *Lucie* gained most points. The American team consisted of *Indian Scout*—Herman F. Whiton, *Lucie*—Briggs Cunningham, *Jil*—J. Johnson, and *Mood*—Phil

Roosevelt. The British team was *Lalage*—Chris Boardman, *Vorsa*—Maurice Clark, *Nike*—J.H. Hume, and *Melita*—Ronald Teacher.

Iyruna

Iyruna came from the Nicholson yard where she was built in 1927 for Sir William P. Burton, KBE. Twelve Metres then cost around £4,800 and raced with a crew of five.

Ruddy Shelduck

A forerunner of the powerboats of today, *Ruddy Shelduck* was built by J.I. Thornycroft at Hampton-on-Thames in 1921. She was owned by the Thornycroft family and makes a fine advertisement of the shipbuilder's craft. The wooden launch was 37ft 7in long and powered with a four-cylinder petrol engine.

Eight Metres

A group of 8 Metre sloops racing off Cowes
during August 1932. From left to right they
are *Unity* K14, *Cutty* K25, *Sagitta* K19 and
Cluaran K6.

White Heather II

This photograph taken in 1932 shows the
yacht's very tall Marconi topmast, fitted in
1920 while she was owned by Sir Charles
Allam. *Britannia*, *Shamrock* and *White
Heather* formed the nucleus of the big class
fleet and raced against each other on many
occasions.

Regina

Originally named *Corona*, this 43-footer was built by Howard & Sons at Maldon in 1911 and designed by F. Shepherd. In 1932 when the photograph was taken *Regina* was owned by Major E. Chesters-Rogerson. Her lines are in contrast to those of the racing yachts of the period, and her 14ft 2in beam and 5ft 8in draft gave her ample accommodation space.

On **Penguin**

A delightful photograph taken in the 1930s of Mr and Mrs Cyril A. Drummond on board their auxiliary schooner *Penguin*. The wooden yacht was 46ft x 10ft 6in x 7ft 2in and had been built on the Hamble in 1913 by Luke & Co.

An Early Dragon

In the early days of the class, Dragons were intended to be cruising boats and had to have a small cabin with a cockpit. This photo was taken in the mid-1930s. After the Second World War they became true racers, though some have made impressive open-sea passages.

Bryony

The 8 Metre *Bryony* on a windy day in August 1936. She had been built by Camper & Nicholson at Gosport in 1909 and designed by R.E. Froude.

Early in the Season

Two studies of the starts of 14-footer races off the Island. The dinghies were sailed by members of the Itchenor Sailing Club and built by H. Felham. The pictures were taken in March in 1933 and 1938.

These predecessors of the International 14s sailed today were designed on practical lines. The open hulls were good for carrying stores when they were used as rowing dinghies. The 14ft hull was the largest that could be sent by train for 6 shillings anywhere in England, and the mast the longest size that could be carried by standard goods waggon, for 1s 6d.

Launch of a J

Following the defeat of *Shamrock V* in the America's Cup races in 1930 and the death of Sir Thomas Lipton, a new challenger came to the fore, T.O.M. Sopwith. His *Endeavour* was launched in 1934 from Camper & Nicholson's, the same yard that had designed and built *Shamrock V*. However, she was to lose to the American defender *Rainbow*.

Whereas Cup racers today are launched in relative privacy, sometimes even secrecy in order to conceal any design advantages, the pre-war launches of Big Class racers attracted the public, as can be seen from the large number of spectators on the steamers in the background. *Endeavour* was 129ft long, 83ft on the waterline and drew nearly 15ft.

Bloodhound and Thanet

The dark-sailed yacht at the left was *Blood-hound*, built by Camper & Nicholson and considered by John Nicholson to be his father's best offshore racer. Launched in 1936 for Isaac Bell who had previously owned *Foxhound*, she had several owners including HM the Queen and HRH Prince Philip. She is still afloat today and I last saw her in Poole Harbour.

This 1936 picture also shows *Thanet* in the foreground.

Jorrocks II

Cruising off the Island in the summer of 1937. *Jorrocks* was built at Burnham-on-Crouch in 1936 by Leslie W. Harris to a design by Maurice Griffiths. She was 30ft 9in long and 9ft 3in beam, and her sweeping sheer and general proportions are pleasing. Her owner was Col Sir Carne Rasch, Bart.

Tally Ho

Making out to deep water. In June 1938 the waters around the Island were soon to see the heavier vessels of war. One hopes *Tally Ho*'s owner, Lord Stanbridge, had a good day's sailing. His 46ft 5in cutter (ex *Alcope Betty*) was built in 1910 by Stow & Son at Shoreham.

Carrina

Kirk shot this canoe-sterned auxiliary schooner on June 4, 1938. *Carrina* was then owned by H.F. Blackborow and had been built by R.J. Perkins & Son at Whitstable in 1929. She was 49ft 5in long; note the wishbone boom between the masts.

Seven II

A fine study of K30 during an 8 Metre race on June 11, 1938. *Seven II* was jointly owned by Major H.W. Hall, MC and F.A. Richards, and built by the Bute Slip Dock Co to a design by A. Mylne & Co of Glasgow.

Thalia

This cruiser was built in 1911 by Harris Bros and she still looks good in this 1938 photograph. Her owner, Capt H.C.R. Brocklebank RN, CBE, can be seen at the tiller.

After the Gun

Kirk was once again at the start of an 8
Metre race off the Island and here he has
captured the scene perfectly. One can
almost hear the gun. *Sagitta* K19 leads the
pack and appears to be benefitting from a
puff of wind.

Maid Marion

The motor yacht *Maid Marion*, designed and
built by Camper & Nicholson's at Gosport in
1908, has a very pleasing and still modern
looking flared bow. The picture was taken in
1938.

Light Wind Start

Eight Metres barely moving in a racing scene taken on June 19, 1938. From left to right can be seen *Saskia* K26, *Seven II* K30, *Sagitta* K19, *Carron II* K31, *Wye* K32 and *Cedora* K28.

Big Class Racing

Herman Andreae, the banker, at the helm of *Endeavour* which he had recently acquired from T.O.M. Sopwith after laying up his *Candida* in 1935. The picture shows one side of the triangular section flat-topped 'Park Avenue' boom. Astern of *Endeavour* is Stephenson's *Velsheda*. (*Glass plate, photographer unknown.*)

Tom Thornycroft steering *Endeavour* during a race in 1936. The long winch handles were 'rowed' by the crew from a seated position. *(Glass plate, photographer unknown.)*

W.F. Stephenson steering his J Class yacht *Velsheda* during a race. Stephenson named her after his three daughters Velma, Sheila and Daphne. Out of the four Js to be built in Britain, *Shamrock V, Endeavour, Endeavour II* and *Velsheda*, she was the only one to be built for racing in home waters. The other three were designed to challenge for the America's Cup. *(Glass plate, photographer unknown.)*